# the AMAZING SPIDER-MAN



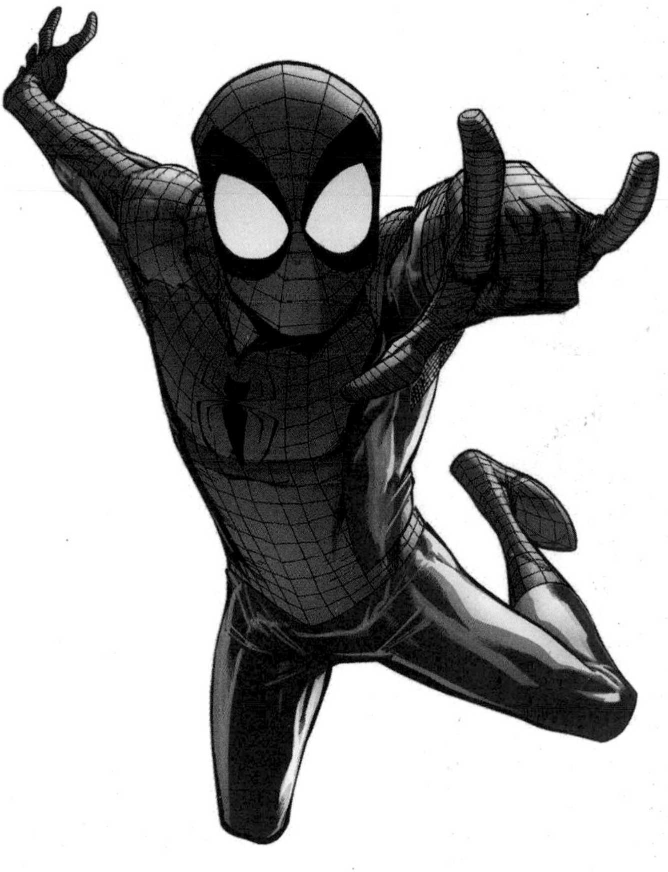

MARVEL

**AMAZING SPIDER-MAN VOL. 1: BEHIND THE MASK.** First printing 2012. ISBN# 978-0-7851-5357-3. Published by MARVEL WORLDWIDE, INC., a subsidiary of MARVEL ENTERTAINMENT, LLC. OFFICE OF PUBLICATION: 135 West 50th Street, New York, NY 10020. Copyright © 2012 Marvel Characters, Inc. All rights reserved. $6.99 per copy in the U.S. and $7.99 in Canada (GST #R127032852); Canadian Agreement #40668537. All characters featured in this issue and the distinctive names and likenesses thereof, and all related indicia are trademarks of Marvel Characters, Inc. No similarity between any of the names, characters, persons, and/or institutions in this magazine with those of any living or dead person or institution is intended, and any such similarity which may exist is purely coincidental. **Printed in the U.S.A.** ALAN FINE, EVP - Office of the President, Marvel Worldwide, Inc. and EVP & CMO Marvel Characters B.V.; DAN BUCKLEY, Publisher & President - Print, Animation & Digital Divisions; JOE QUESADA, Chief Creative Officer; TOM BREVOORT, SVP of Publishing; DAVID BOGART, SVP of Operations & Procurement, Publishing; RUWAN JAYATILLEKE, SVP & Associate Publisher, Publishing; C.B. CEBULSKI, SVP of Creator & Content Development; DAVID GABRIEL, SVP of Publishing Sales & Circulation; MICHAEL PASCIULLO, SVP of Brand Planning & Communications; JIM O'KEEFE, VP of Operations & Logistics; DAN CARR, Executive Director of Publishing Technology; SUSAN CRESPI, Editorial Operations Manager; ALEX MORALES, Publishing Operations Manager; STAN LEE, Chairman Emeritus. For information regarding advertising in Marvel Comics or on Marvel.com, please contact John Dokes, SVP Integrated Sales and Marketing, at jdokes@marvel.com. For Marvel subscription inquiries, please call 800-217-9158. **Manufactured between 4/16//2012 and 5/7/2012 by R.R. DONNELLEY, INC., CRAWFORDSVILLE, IN, USA.**

10 9 8 7 6 5 4 3 2 1

# the AMAZING SPIDER-MAN

## BEHIND THE MASK

Writer
**JOE CARAMAGNA**
Comic Artists
**SCOTT KOBLISH** (pages 1-7)
**GIANCARLO CARACUZZO** (pages 8-14)
Colorist
**SOTOCOLOR**
Letterer
**JOE CARAMAGNA**
Cover Artists
**PATRICK SCHERBERGER** with **EDGAR DELGADO**
Spot Illustrations
**SCOTT KOBLISH** with **SOTOCOLOR**
and **PAUL RYAN, JOHN ROMITA & DAMION SCOTT**
Comic Editors
**NATHAN COSBY & JORDAN D. WHITE**
Prose Editor
**CORY LEVINE**

Assistant Editors: Alex Starbuck & Nelson Ribeiro
Editors, Special Projects: Jennifer Grünwald & Mark D. Beazley
Senior Editor, Special Projects: Jeff Youngquist
Senior Vice President of Sales: David Gabriel
Associate Publisher & SVP of Print, Animation and Digital Media: Ruwan Jayatilleke
SVP of Brand Planning & Communications: Michael Pasciullo
Book Design: Marie Drion & Joe Frontirre

Editor In Chief: Axel Alonso
Chief Creative Officer: Joe Quesada
Publisher: Dan Buckley
Executive Producer: Alan Fine

# SPIDER-MAN

The former professional wrestler turned super hero learned the hard way that with great power must come great responsibility. To make up for his past mistakes, he has vowed to protect New York City from all those who wish to do harm.

# PETER PARKER

Raised from childhood by his Uncle Ben and Aunt May, he always dreamed of becoming a scientist like his late father. But after a lab accident — and a radioactive spider bite — grants him special powers, he discovers his true calling.

# UNCLE BEN

As Peter's father figure, Uncle Ben has taught him many life lessons. But the most important one of all is that "with great power there must also come great responsibility."

# AUNT MAY

After the death of Peter's parents, May Parker and her husband, Ben, raised their nephew as if he were their own child.

# FLASH THOMPSON

Eugene "Flash" Thompson is Midtown High's star football player but also its biggest bully. Little does he know his favorite victim, Peter Parker, is really New York City's greatest super hero!

## J. JONAH JAMESON

The publisher of the Daily Bugle brings attention to his floundering newspaper by going after New York City's beloved costumed vigilante.

## CAPTAIN STACY

A longtime veteran of the police department, Captain Stacy keeps law and order in New York City.

# THE VULTURE

Adrian Toomes spent his life as an engineer but never felt appreciated by his employers. After he was fired, he decided to use his greatest invention, the Vulture harness, to gain the respect he felt he always deserved.

# SANDMAN

While on the run from the police, a chemical accident left criminal Flint Marko with the ability to turn his body into sand.

# DOCTOR OCTOPUS

Dr. Otto Octavius is a world-renowned, yet accident-prone, nuclear physicist. After one accident too many leaves him melded to a set of four additional mechanical arms, he becomes Spider-Man's most formidable super villain!

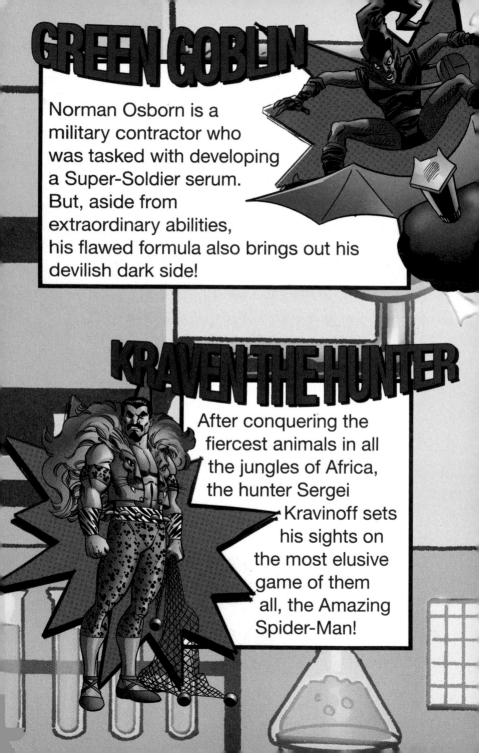

# GREEN GOBLIN

Norman Osborn is a military contractor who was tasked with developing a Super-Soldier serum. But, aside from extraordinary abilities, his flawed formula also brings out his devilish dark side!

# KRAVEN THE HUNTER

After conquering the fiercest animals in all the jungles of Africa, the hunter Sergei Kravinoff sets his sights on the most elusive game of them all, the Amazing Spider-Man!

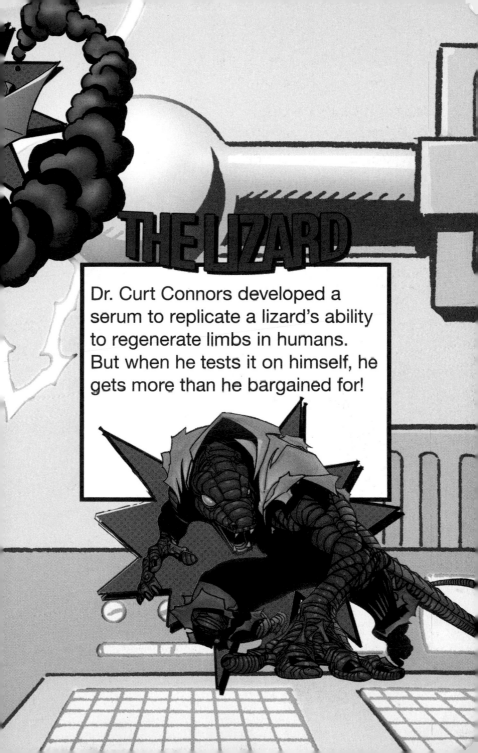

# THE LIZARD

Dr. Curt Connors developed a serum to replicate a lizard's ability to regenerate limbs in humans. But when he tests it on himself, he gets more than he bargained for!

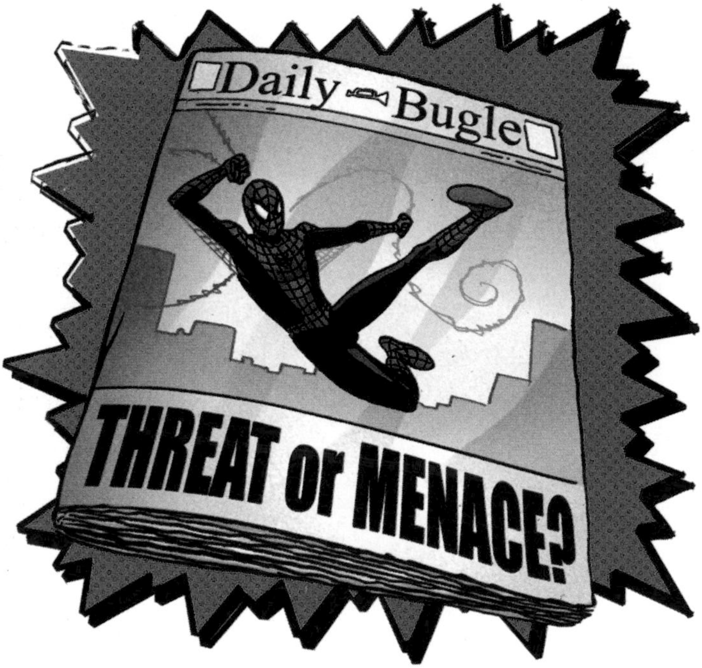
Daily Bugle
THREAT or MENACE?

CHAPTER 1

One sunny morning in New York City, mild-mannered teenager Peter Parker walked through the early morning rush hour with his head hanging low, but secretly he was smiling on the inside. On any other day, Peter would be shuffling through the halls of Midtown High, trying not to be noticed...but this was no ordinary day. While other teenage boys were interested in cars and sports, Peter was content with the subway and didn't know a hockey puck from a doughnut. What Peter loved most of all were his class trips to Empire State University's science labs where he could forget about his high school problems and dream about what life would be like as a real-life physicist!

"Petey, Petey!" a voice called from behind.

It was his Uncle Ben trotting across the street, waving a sheet of paper. "Petey, wait! You forgot this...huff...I think you need this to...puff..." he said, out of breath. "I think you need this to get in."

"You came all this way for my permission slip?" Peter asked, taking the paper from him. "I probably could have had Mr. Ditko call you--

"Oh..."

"What?"

"You signed it above 'parent' and not 'legal guardian.'"

Uncle Ben blushed. Sometimes he actually forgot that Peter wasn't his actual son because he and Aunt May had raised him since he was a baby. But the last thing he wanted was for Peter to think he was trying to replace his real mom and dad, who were lost in an accident many years ago.

"Oh! I'm sorry. If you have a pen, I'll fix--"

"No," Peter said as he smiled and shoved it into his backpack. "I'm sure it'll be fine."

Uncle Ben understood, and smiled back. He thought about how much Peter had grown up since he and Aunt May first took him in. Now, sixteen years later, Peter was a happy and healthy honors student who helped Aunt May with the chores and always did the right thing. He was a good boy.

"Um, Uncle Ben..." Peter said. "...is that all?"

"Oh! Yes! I wouldn't want to

embarrass you in front of your friends!" Uncle Ben waved and began his long walk back. "Have fun, Petey! I know how much you've been looking forward to this day!"

That's right! If Peter was going to get a good spot at the radioactivity demonstration he had to hurry. He moved quickly, but as soon as he was out of Uncle Ben's sight--

"Hey, guys, look! It's 'Peeeeetey.'"

Flash Thompson and two of his friends from Midtown High's football team were hanging out on the corner. Flash was the school's star quarterback, and compared to Peter, he was the size of an ox. "Is it grandpa's big day out from the old folks' home?" Flash teased.

"He's my uncle," Peter muttered and continued on his way without making eye contact.

But Flash wasn't finished yet and followed him as he walked. "Oh, that's right. I forgot," he said. "Hey, did you guys know that 'Petey' doesn't have any parents?" Peter tried to ignore

them, but the more he did, the louder Flash got. "It's true! His parents threw themselves under a bus or something. Even they couldn't stand to be around him.

"Isn't that right, 'Peeeeeeetey'?"

Flash's buddies roared with laughter, but Peter didn't think it was funny at all. It was one thing to be called names like "Pete The Science Geek" or "Puny Parker," but this time Flash was making fun of Uncle Ben... and his parents! He should have ignored them, but he couldn't stand to listen to any more of it.

"Shut up, Flash." And as soon as

the words left his mouth, he knew he'd made a mistake. There was no way Flash would let him get away with embarrassing him in front of the football team.

"WHAT DID YOU SAY?" Flash shoved Peter so hard in the back it knocked his glasses off his face. He tried to stay on his feet, but landed hard on the sidewalk. A fireball of pain exploded from his knees. The bullies surrounded him. Flash squeezed his hands into fists. "Get up!" he shouted, "Get up and let's see how tough you are!" The last thing Peter wanted was to have to fight someone as big and

strong as Flash Thompson. Instead,
he curled up on the ground, nursing
his sore knees, and closed his eyes and
wished the bullies would go away, when
suddenly--

"HEY!" a familiar voice shouted
from far away. "Leave him alone!"

When Flash saw Uncle Ben
running toward them, he stuffed
his hands in his pockets and quickly
walked away. "I know you! You're the
Thompson boy. *Eugene* Thompson,"

Uncle Ben said. Peter had never heard anybody call Flash by his real name; even all of the teachers called him "Flash!" "Your parents are going to hear from me when I get home."

Flash shrugged his shoulders. "He started it," he said with a wave.

Uncle Ben helped Peter up to his feet. "Are you all right, Petey?" he asked. But Peter wasn't all right. He was crying.

"WHY DID YOU DO THAT?" he shouted.

"Petey, what--?"

"If I just *stay down,* they get bored with it and leave me alone. But now...I'll never be able to live this down. EVER!"

"Peter," Uncle Ben said, trying to

calm him down, "you can't let guys like Thompson walk all over you like that. You have to *stand up* to him. If he knows you're afraid, he'll--"

"You don't know how it is, okay? Just go away!"

"But, Petey--"

"I HATE YOU!"

Uncle Ben gasped. Peter had never shouted at him like that before, it was like a punch to his gut! Peter grabbed his backpack and ran toward the science lab as fast as he could, with his broken glasses in his hand. Uncle Ben wanted to run after him, but he knew he'd already done too much. He embarrassed Peter in front of his classmates, but he was only trying to protect him. It was all he knew how to do.

CHAPTER
2

"And now, here's a brief demonstration of how we experiment with radioactivity here in the lab." Dr. Lee, a physicist at Empire State University, motioned to Mr. Ditko, head of Midtown High's science department, to push a button on the console in front of him. The room full of students "*oohed*" and "*ahhed*" as a cluster of large machines behind the safety glass beeped and buzzed with colorful lights.

"The ionization of atoms is known to cause cancer in living cells," Dr. Lee said. "Hence the six-inch glass separating us from the equipment." The scientist flipped a switch and the largest machine in the room roared to life. An electrical beam zapped from one contact to the other, covering the room in a glow of blue light. Dr. Lee pressed more buttons and the blue electricity crackled loudly as the two contacts on the machine moved closer together. "But it's also been known to cause *anomalies* in them as well."

Usually, a scientific demonstration this remarkable would easily grab Peter Parker's attention, but he wasn't in the mood today. His glasses broke in the scuffle outside, so he couldn't see very well anyway, but mostly, he felt badly for yelling at Uncle Ben. He wasn't angry with him, but he

was really angry at himself for letting
Flash humiliate him. And every time
he tried to forget about it, he heard
the whispers from the back of the
room.

"That old man better not say a
word to my mom," said Flash. "If I
get grounded and miss the game
this weekend, I'll take it out on puny
Parker for the rest of the year!"

As Dr. Lee lectured, a small spider

lowered itself from its web down into the energy beam between the crackling contacts. Once the beams hit it, the spider jumped wildly! It kicked its legs back and forth, but couldn't wriggle free. The blue light crackled louder and brighter.

"We experiment with bacteria, fungi, insects, and *arachnids*..." Dr. Lee continued, "...trying to create anomalies here in the lab so we can study them to find out *why* they occur so that we can learn to control them."

"I say we give him a warning shot now..." Flash said from the back of the room, "...so he knows I mean business."

Suddenly, the lights on the control panel flickered red. The machines roared louder. "Wait, something seems to be--" Dr. Lee began, but the control panel exploded in a shower of sparks! The machines began to smoke!

"Everyone get back!" Dr. Lee shouted.

The light flared so brightly, the students shielded their eyes. "Come on, guys, let's get out of here," Flash shouted and pushed the door open. Mr. Ditko ordered the whole class to follow him out to the parking lot, but Peter was mesmerized by what was happening. This was real science!

Suddenly--SKRASSH!--the machine behind the window exploded, spraying the room with a million pieces of glass! Peter put his arms in front of his face to protect himself, but he felt a sharp pinch in the back of his hand. Broken glass! "OWWW!" he shrieked.

Except it *wasn't*. Peter looked at his hand and saw the little black spider that soaked up all of the radiation in the experiment. He must have been thrown by the explosion and, in desperation, bit into the first thing that he landed on.

"Son, are you okay?" Dr. Lee asked as he pulled him out by the arm. Peter watched the spider stiffen and fall dead to the floor. "Come ON!" Dr. Lee shouted.

"Class, stay together while we call the paramedics," Mr. Ditko said, but as his classmates gathered on the sidewalk, Peter kept walking. He wasn't feeling well; he was dizzy and his legs felt rubbery. "Hey, wait!" Mr. Ditko shouted. "You can't leave until we make sure you're all right!" But Peter wouldn't listen. His stomach was in knots. The spider bite on his hand throbbed. He needed to get away.

"Hey, Flash, where's puny Parker going?" one of the bullies whispered.

"Nowhere we can't get to him. Come on," Flash said.

Across the street, Peter escaped into a secluded alley lined with trash cans. He felt sick to his stomach and couldn't hold it anymore! He grabbed the lid off of one of them and..."BLARRGGHH!"

*What's happening?* he wondered. *Am I allergic to spider bites? Could it be--?*

"What's wrong, Petey? Not feeling well?" Peter could tell by the way Flash and his buddies came into the alley that they weren't there to talk; they were there to finish what they started. He tried to speak, but couldn't. "Not so brave when the old man's not around, huh?" said Flash as he pounded a fist into his open palm to show Peter what he was in for.

Peter was no match for them on a good day, but now? His legs felt brittle, and he could barely stand. He quickly looked behind him and saw plenty of room to run but didn't know if his legs could handle it. Flash reached out to grab him...and Peter took off into the alley as fast as he could! Suddenly, his legs weren't shaky anymore. They tingled! They had new life. They had *power*!

"GET HIM!" Flash shouted to his buddies, and they gave chase! But the faster the bullies' legs moved, so did Peter's! They couldn't keep up with the new power in Peter's legs. *Where was it coming from?*

But when Peter turned the corner to make his final getaway, he ran straight into a fence! He was trapped and he could hear Flash's footsteps coming around the corner. He'd never be able to climb a fence this tall before Flash got to him. He was a goner for sure!

Peter felt a tingle in his knees. With time running out, without even thinking, he bent down deeply and pushed his sneakers off the pavement with all the force he could muster.

Flash turned the corner and ran straight into the fence! His goons followed so closely behind, they ran right into his back. Flash grabbed the chain link with his fingers and looked around, but didn't see Peter anywhere. He wasn't used to looking foolish, and his face turned red with rage. "Where

did he go?" shouted Flash, but his friends just shrugged.

"He couldn't have gotten too far," said one of the other bullies. "There must be some other *secret* way out. Yeah, that's it. Come on, Flash." Flash turned to leave but looked over his shoulder one last time to make sure Peter wasn't just hiding somewhere. He didn't know how he got away, but the next time he saw him, he was going to teach him a lesson.

Meanwhile, twenty-five feet above the ground, Peter Parker let out the big breath he had been holding to stay quiet. Way above the alley where Flash was just standing, Peter clung to the side of a brick wall with just his bare hands! He couldn't explain how it happened: With nowhere else to go, he jumped as high as he could — and kept going and going — right over the fence! And when he stuck his hand out to grab onto something, it stuck to the brick wall! He placed his other hand on it, and it stuck too!

But after Flash left and the alley was clear, Peter was afraid to move a muscle. What if he fell to the ground and broke his arm, or worse?! What if he *couldn't* move and was glued in place? But he couldn't just stay there all night; he had to try. He closed his eyes and braced for the worst as he peeled his left hand away. Then,

some brittle mortar broke from under the soles of his shoes and he slipped! "Whoa!" Peter shouted... except he didn't fall! The fingers of his right hand were still firmly fixed in place, holding safely to the wall.

Peter put his left hand back on the wall and it stuck again. This time he let go with his right hand, reached up higher and stuck it back to the wall. Slowly, he was moving hand over hand, foot after foot and before he knew it, he was crawling up the wall like a bug! *How is this possible?* Peter wondered. *And what other things can I do?*

"I know it hasn't been that long, but it's not like Peter not to call," Uncle Ben said quietly into the phone.

"I appreciate your help anyway, Captain Stacy. I'll keep calling around."

Uncle Ben peeked his head out of the kitchen to the chair where Aunt May had been sitting for the past few hours, watching the news reports of the explosion. He tried to keep the phone calls quiet on account of her heart condition, but he knew by the tears in her eyes that she had been listening to him. He couldn't give up. He scanned the list of names and phone numbers for someone — anyone — who might have seen his nephew, when he heard a sudden noise at the front door. "Peter!" he heard Aunt May say.

Uncle Ben sprang into the foyer but Peter was already sprinting up the stairs to his bedroom. "Peter! Thank goodness!" he called out. "Where have you been? When we heard about the explosion--"

"I'm fine! I'm...going to bed. Good night!" he shouted down the stairs before slamming his bedroom door shut.

Peter leaned his tired head against the wall and wiped the cold sweat from his forehead. So many questions swam through his head: *What was happening to him? Was it the spider bite? Was it the*

*radiation? Was it both? Was it temporary?*
*And* — gulp — *could this possibly kill him?*

He pushed his microscope aside to clear some room on his desk, then grabbed a pile of pamphlets and newspaper articles from his bottom drawer and threw them down in front of him. He was looking for answers, but deep down inside he knew there wasn't a science journal in the world that could provide them. He was one of those *anomalies* that Dr. Lee was talking about.

"Um...Peter?" a friendly voice outside of his door said with a gentle knock.

But Peter didn't dare reply. What could he say? What possible explanation could he have for where he had been all this time? Why was he pale and sweaty? There was nothing he could do but stay quiet and hope that his uncle would take the hint and go away. After all, he always could tell when Peter was lying. Or sick.

"Petey? Can you open this door, please?"

No, not *sick*! He couldn't have been sick. He felt *great*! He felt stronger than he had ever felt before, like he could move a mountain! And those other things he could do were *amazing*! Somehow, the radioactive bite gave him the proportional strength and abilities of a spider! *Let's see Flash Thompson come after me now*, Peter thought.

"Peter, can we talk about what happened?" asked Uncle Ben through the door. But Peter still ignored him. He couldn't tell anyone about this, not even Uncle Ben and Aunt May. If anyone found out, they'd put him in a laboratory and study him like he was some kind of freak. But this was his big chance to be something more than "Pete The Science Geek" or "Puny Parker." He needed a mask... and a costume. From then on he would be known as the AMAZING SPIDER-MAN!

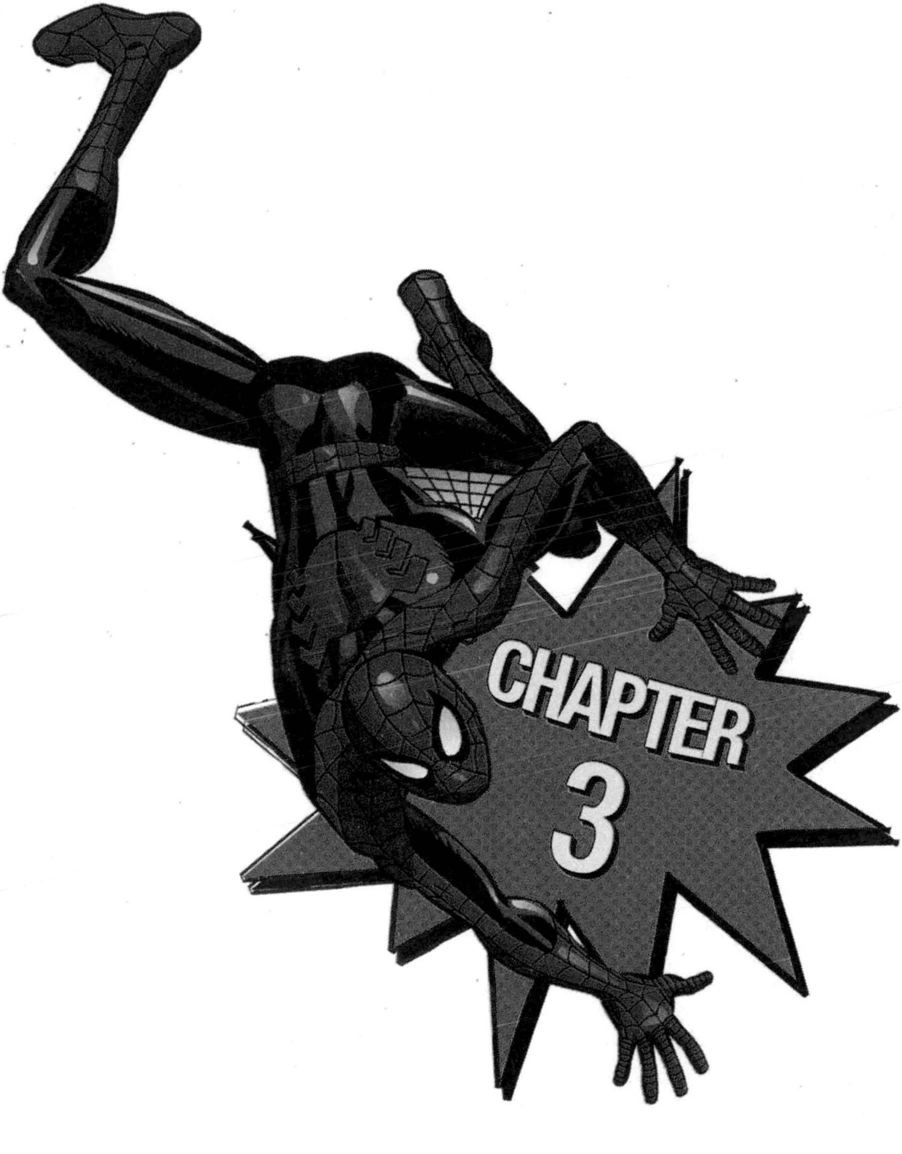
CHAPTER
3

Two weeks later, Uncle Ben and Peter still hadn't talked. Uncle Ben felt badly that he had embarrassed Peter in front of his classmates, but that didn't excuse Peter for yelling at him the way that he did. Someone had to break the ice, so Uncle Ben decided to apologize for his part in it. But every morning Peter skipped family breakfast and then stayed out after school until the evening. When he *was* home, Peter locked himself in his room and didn't come out or talk to anyone.

One night, Uncle Ben decided to give it a shot. For sixteen years they were the best of friends. He couldn't let one bad experience ruin their relationship. "Peter?" he said with a knock on the locked bedroom door.

There was no answer, so Uncle Ben knocked again. "Peter? Do you want to watch the wrestling match with us?" he said a bit louder. This time he put his ear against the door, but there was no sound from the other side. Uncle Ben frowned. "I guess you need a little more time," he said. "I just want you to know...I'm sorry about what happened. You mean the world to me."

But what Uncle Ben didn't know was that earlier that evening, Peter had snuck out through his bedroom window, and he had been talking to an empty room.

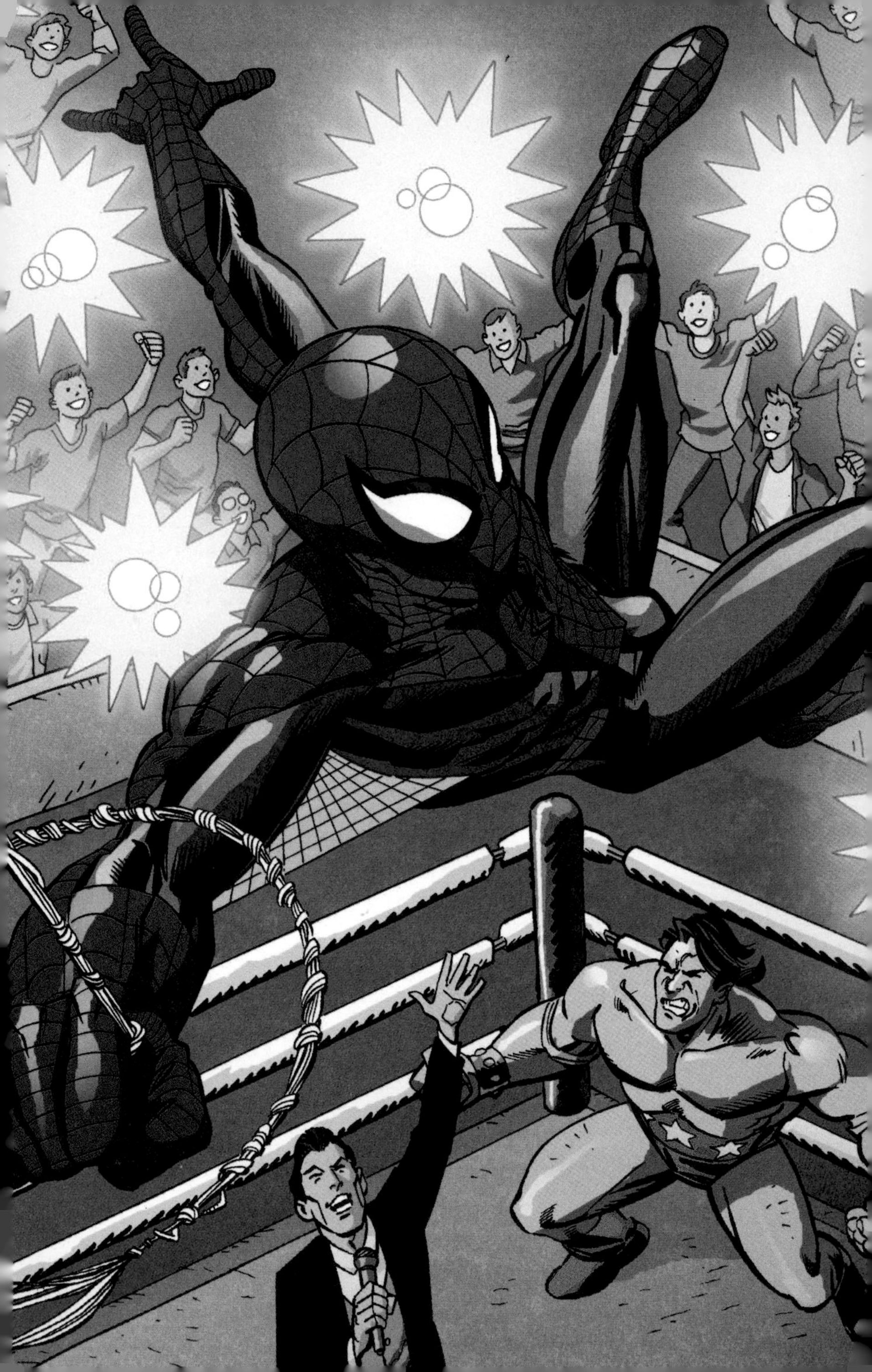

"And now, ladies and gentleman, it's time for our MAIN EVENT!" The ring announcer proudly declared to an arena filled with rowdy wrestling fans.

"In this corner, weighing two hundred forty-two pounds...PRETTY BOY TROY!" Troy's long, dark locks shook as he bounced from foot to foot and blew kisses to the crowd that booed him heartily. After all, Troy wasn't the man they'd paid to see.

"And his opponent..." Before he could finish his sentence, the fans howled! They were eager to see the new superstar who, in just a few short days, had taken the wrestling world by storm. The announcer pulled the microphone closer to his mouth to yell over their cheers, "Weighing one hundred and fifty-five pounds...the AMAAAAAAZING SPIDER-MAN!"

Cameras flashed all around the arena! The spectators jumped out of their seats as the most unusual wrestler they had ever seen swung down from the ceiling in a bright red and blue costume with a spider-web pattern. Because he wore a full face mask, nobody had any idea that this wrestler was really just teenaged science student, Peter Parker!

When the bell sounded, Pretty Boy Troy lunged from his corner to catch the fan-favorite by surprise, but Spider-Man side-stepped him with ease, sending Troy face-first into the opposite corner. Troy turned around and threw a heavy punch, but again Spider-Man dodged the strike with a high jump. He was by far the most agile fighter the adoring crowd had ever seen! When Spider-Man pushed Troy down to the mat with a kick to the star on the seat of his wrestling trunks, the fans roared with laughter! Troy, very embarrassed, sprang back up to his feet, made sure his hair was still in place, then lunged again! But Spider-Man kicked the handsome wrestler in the stomach and knocked the wind right out of him!

"Take it easy, kid," Troy grunted. "You really hurt me that time!" But the fans weren't there to see him take it easy, and urged him on, chanting, "Spidey! Spidey!"

"But listen to the them! They're eating it up!" Spider-Man said. He jumped high over Troy's head and landed on the other side of him. When he turned around, Spider-Man dropkicked him in the chest, sending Troy hard into the corner of the ring! "And speaking of 'eating,' what did *you* eat today? Your breath smells like you brushed your teeth with kitty litter!"

Before Troy could reply, Spider-Man pressed a small button in the palm of his hand, and stringy, sticky goop — like a spider's web — sprayed from his own special invention, a web-shooting bracelet hidden beneath his red and blue gloves. The webbing went all over Troy's mouth! He grabbed at it, but it stuck to him like glue. Spidey, still holding the other end of the web, yanked it hard over his shoulder, lifting Troy right up off the mat and clear over the ropes. Troy fell hard onto the floor!

The match was over! Spider-Man was the winner! The audience thundered in applause and again chanted, "Spidey! Spidey!" Underneath the mask, young Peter Parker smiled with delight. Everyone in the stadium adored him!

Well, *almost* everyone. Pretty Boy Troy, his face covered in webs, struggled to get up to his feet. For the first time in his long wrestling career he was made to look like a fool. Spider-Man didn't wrestle the way they had planned and he humiliated Troy just to make himself look better.

"But, Mr. Barnaby...that's not fair!"

"Life ain't fair. You know the rule, kid," said the wrestling promoter, as he removed large stacks of money from a pile on his desk and dropped them into a laundry bag. "I'm not paying you until I get your *real* name on a real *contract*."

"But my identity is a secret! Nobody can ever find out who I really am!"

"Sorry, Spidey," Barnaby shrugged, "but you don't get what *you* want until I get what *I* want."

A janitor, who was in the promoter's office mopping the floor, couldn't help but overhear. The scar over his left eye bounced as he cackled. He'd never seen such a big pile of cash after just one show and he knew a shrewd promoter like Mr. Barnaby wasn't going to give that up quite so easily.

Mr. Barnaby slipped on his dark glasses and laughed along with him. Their laughter reminded Peter of Flash Thompson and his buddies, and Peter couldn't stand it. Even now, after all the great things he could do, they still treated him like "Puny Parker."

In a rage, Spider-Man grabbed Mr. Barnaby by the collar of his flashy

sport coat and lifted the heavy man
high into the air with ease! The janitor
suddenly didn't think it was so funny
anymore and went back to taking
out the trash. "I won't be bullied ever
again!" said Spider-Man. "Pay me what
you owe me!"

"All right, f-fine. T-take your share,
just don't hurt me!" Barnaby said.

*That felt good*, Peter thought, as he strutted down the hall from Mr. Barnaby's office in his Spider-Man costume. For the first time in his life, he stood up for himself. And after the match, the fans, the money, and his newfound nerve...it was a great day.

"E-excuse me, Spider-Man," a young man said from the elevator doors. Except it wasn't just any young man... it was Flash Thompson! And his bully buddies were with him! But they didn't look the way they did when they were picking on Peter. Next to Spider-Man, they looked shorter and uncertain. They looked *weak*. "Can I have y-your autograph?"

Spider-Man looked at the pen and paper in Flash's hand, but didn't take it. He decided to have some fun instead. "I know you," he said, disguising his voice so they wouldn't recognize him. "You're that quarterback who took Midtown High to the state championship. Flash Thompson!"

Flash's eyes lit up! "Yeah! That's me!" he said, standing up taller and confidently. *Now* he looked more like the bully Peter knew so well. "We almost won that game too!"

"Almost?" Spider-Man mocked. "Sorry, kid..."

With a mere flick of his wrist, using great spider-strength, Spider-Man shoved Flash hard into the elevator buttons on the wall. "Ooof!"

"...but I don't sign autographs for losers."

The elevator doors opened wide, but before Spider-Man could get in, he heard someone down the hall shout, "HEY! STOP HIM!"

Spider-Man and Flash turned to

see the janitor running toward them from Mr. Barnaby's office. In one hand was the laundry bag full of money and in his other hand...a gun! Mr. Barnaby chased after him, but couldn't keep up.

"Pardon me," the janitor said as he slipped past the teenagers and into the open elevator. As the doors closed, Spider-Man watched the scar above his eye bounce with laughter again as the thief escaped.

"What's the matter with you?" Mr. Barnaby shouted at the web-slinger. "Couldn't you just trip him or grab him or something?!"

"Sorry, Mr. Barnaby," he answered, "Life ain't fair." As Peter walked away from Mr. Barnaby, Flash Thompson and the bullies, he smiled under his mask again. *This isn't just a great day,* he thought, *it's the greatest day of my life!*

CHAPTER
4

Peter put his regular clothes on over his Spider-Man costume and stuffed the mask and his winnings from the match into his pocket for the walk home from the arena. It was the first time in a long time that he was proud to be himself again. *Oh, if*

*only Uncle Ben could have seen that*, he thought. *He would have been so proud!*

But Peter hadn't spoken to Uncle Ben since the confrontation with Flash at the University. So many exciting things had happened since then, but without Uncle Ben to share them with, they seemed a little less...special. He decided that when he got home, he'd apologize for the way he'd acted. *Actually*, thought Peter, *I should tell him all about it — the spider, the powers, the wrestling — everything. I bet he'd get a real kick out of it.*

But when Peter rounded the corner to his street, he saw two police cars and an ambulance parked in front of his apartment building! It gave him a very bad feeling in his gut. *It must be Aunt May's heart!* "Aunt May! Uncle Ben!" he shouted, pushing past some people who had gathered out front. Peter ran for the door, but a large police officer with a bushy mustache stretched out his arm to block his path.

"Whoa! Sorry, son, you can't go in there!"

"Where's my aunt?" Peter asked.

"Oh! You must be Peter! I'm Officer Keating. We've been calling all

over for you."

"Where's Aunt May?" Peter
repeated.

Officer Keating placed his hands
on Peter's shoulders. "Your Aunt May
is fine, son. She's over at the Watsons'
house." Peter put his hand over his
heart and let out a sigh of relief. But
Officer Keating didn't look as relieved.
If Aunt May was over at the Watsons'
then where was--

"Uncle Ben?" Peter asked.

Officer Keating bowed his head
and frowned. Peter's heart started
beating so loudly, he could barely
make out the policeman's words. It was
a burglar. He had a gun. Uncle Ben

thought Peter was asleep in his room and tried to protect him. The gun went off and--

The officer looked away. Peter collapsed inside. His arms and legs trembled. His eyes filled with tears. He couldn't believe it. Uncle Ben was gone. He was *really* gone. All because he was trying to protect *Peter.*

"But don't worry," Officer Keating

continued as he gripped Peter's shoulders tightly. "We found the guy. We got him cornered in an old warehouse on the waterfront.

"Now, you'd better go see your Aunt May, she's worried sick about you. There's nothing you can do here."

Officer Keating was right, there was nothing Peter Parker could have done. But Spider-Man can do all kinds of amazing things.

The old, empty warehouse on the Hudson River came alive in the glow of the flashing red lights of a dozen police cars. A lifetime on the job had taught Captain

George Stacy to stay patient during times like this, so he ordered his officers to surround the building and keep their distance — the burglar inside had a gun and was willing to use it. Instead, he'd try everything that he could to draw him out first

before risking anyone's safety with a raid. "Don't be foolish," Captain Stacy said, his voice electronically amplified through the night sky by a megaphone. "There's nowhere for you to go. Come out peacefully, and I promise you won't be hurt."

Inside the warehouse, the burglar wiped away the dust from a dirty old window and saw that Captain Stacy was right; there were police officers everywhere. But he knew as long as he stayed put, he'd be safe. Nobody would dare come after him, would they?

The burglar's eyes jumped as a sudden creaking sound came from the shadows in the ceiling's rafters. He raised his gun slowly. Were there policemen on the roof? Was Captain Stacy just a distraction? Suddenly a voice called out:

CRICK!

"MURDERER!"

The burglar spun around and blindly fired his gun twice into the darkness! Without knowing if he'd hit anything, he ran away as fast as he could, but a figure in red and blue dropped from out of the shadows to block his path! It was Spider-Man!

janitor who stole Mr. Barnaby's bag full of money. The same janitor that Peter let escape into the elevator because he was too busy getting revenge on Flash Thompson. That same janitor had shot Uncle Ben.

Peter dropped to the floor, then pulled the spider-mask from his face and began to cry. What a fool he had been! Had he stopped him earlier when he took Mr. Barnaby's money, the janitor would have been behind bars and unable to do what he did to Uncle Ben. It was all Peter's fault!

Outside, Captain Stacy crawled out from behind a police car. He hadn't heard gunshots from inside the building for several minutes, so he felt it was safe to get back up. *Slowly.* He wasn't sure what had happened, but he held a finger to his mouth to make sure the officers stayed quiet as he tried to listen for any movement.

Suddenly, something big crashed through the window and landed hard on the pavement in front of the police. Captain Stacy and a few officers ran over and saw that it was the burglar; he was wrapped from head to toe in what looked like a thick spider's web! *Who could have done this?* the captain wondered. And when he looked up into the sky, he saw exactly who — that professional wrestler he had seen on television, the Spider-Man! He watched him swing away on a web and disappear into the Manhattan skyline.

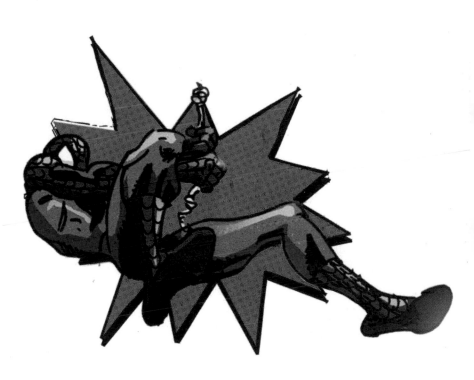

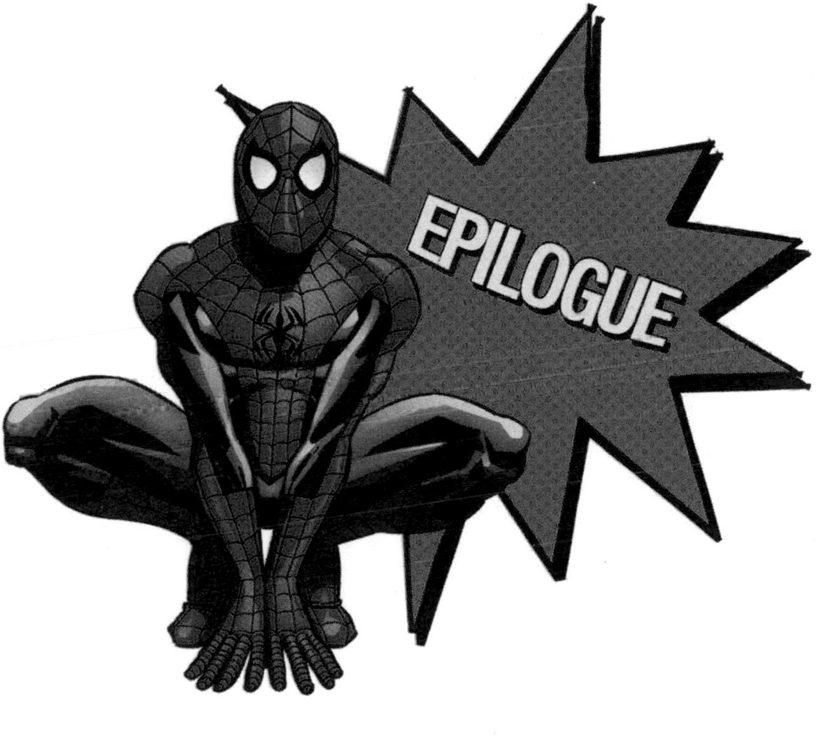
EPILOGUE

Three days later, a long black car pulled to the curb in front of the Parkers' apartment building. Peter, wearing a suit and tie, stepped out first and reached back to take the outstretched hand of Aunt May, who was catching her tears in a handkerchief. It was all over. Uncle Ben was gone; now it was time to step inside and start his new life as the man of the house.

After much thinking, Peter realized he was wrong to think Uncle Ben would have been proud of the way he acted. By using his new abilities to overpower Flash Thompson and Mr. Barnaby, he was no better than they were. He was being selfish and had learned the hard way that with great power must come great responsibility. To make it up to Uncle Ben, he had to make things right.

Peter heard the distant wail of a police siren. Something was happening.

Now wearing his red and blue Spider-Man costume, he climbed out of his bedroom window and into the alley. He touched his sticky fingers to the wall and began to climb to the roof to get a better look at where the police were headed. His uncle was right: In times of trouble, he couldn't stay down, he had to *stand up*. New York City needed someone with his special gifts to help make sure what happened to Uncle Ben would never happen to anyone else. New York City needed a hero like the Amazing Spider-Man!

THE END

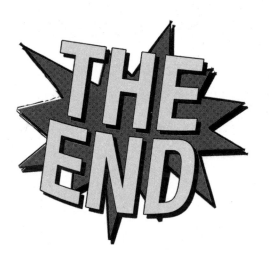

J FINE

**PETEY!**

**PETEY! WAIT!**

YOUR PERMISSION SLIP! I FIGURED YOU'D NEED IT TO GET INTO THE UNIVERSITY.

OH! YOU CAME ALL THIS WAY? I COULD'VE JUST HAD MR. DITKO CALL YOU OR SOMETHING--

WHAT?

OH...

YOU CIRCLED *"PARENT"* NOT *"GUARDIAN"* UNDER THE SIGNATURE.

OH! I DIDN'T-- IF YOU HAVE A *PEN*, I COULD...

NO, I'M SURE IT'S...

IT'S *FINE.* THANKS.

IS THAT IT?

OH! RIGHT!

WOULDN'T WANT TO EMBARRASS YOU IN FRONT OF YOUR FRIENDS!

HAVE FUN, PETEY! I KNOW HOW YOU'VE BEEN LOOKING FORWARD TO THIS!

*"PETEY"*?

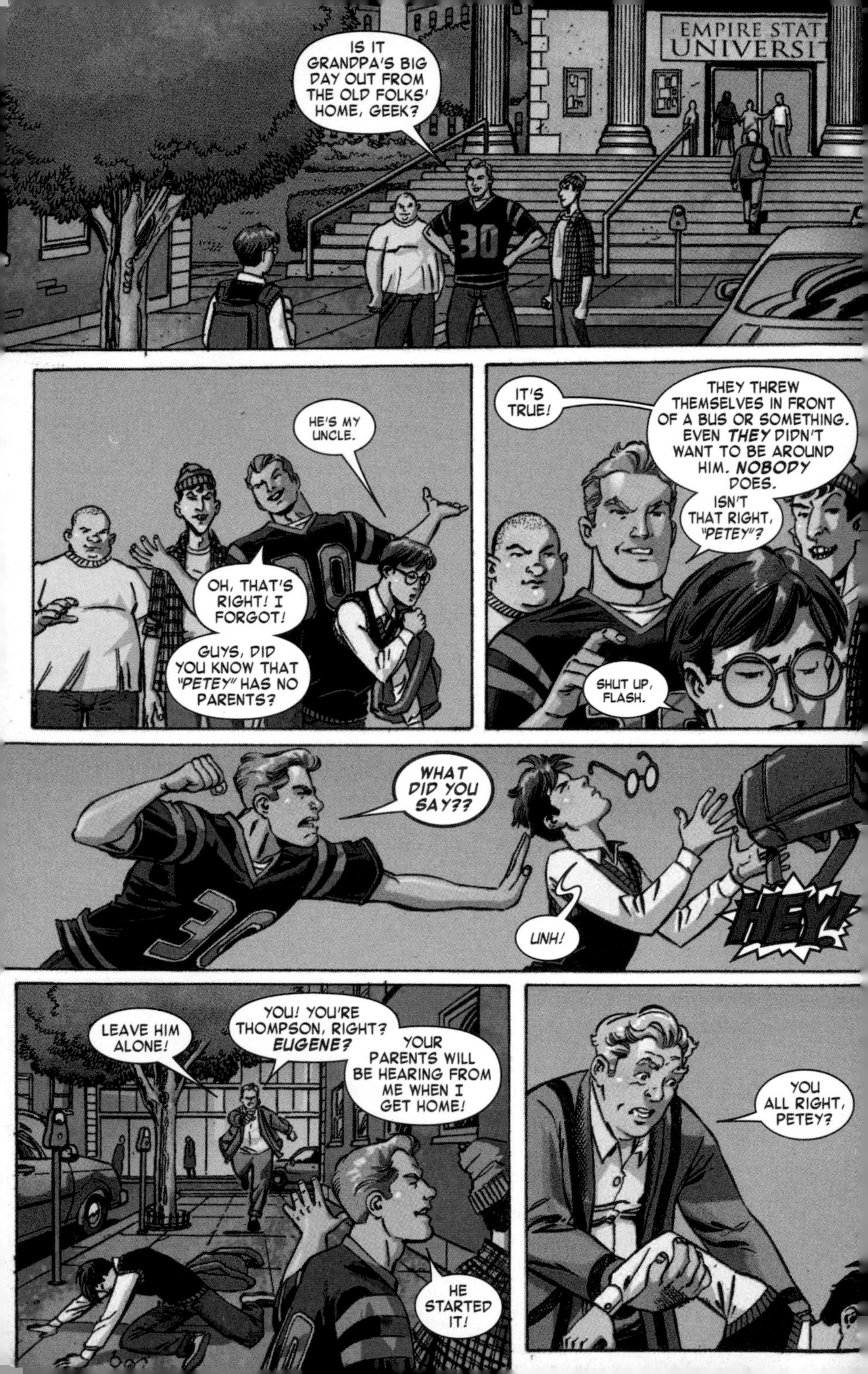
EMPIRE STATE
UNIVERSIT
IS IT GRANDPA'S BIG DAY OUT FROM THE OLD FOLKS' HOME, GEEK?
HE'S MY UNCLE.
OH, THAT'S RIGHT! I FORGOT!
GUYS, DID YOU KNOW THAT "PETEY" HAS NO PARENTS?
IT'S TRUE!
THEY THREW THEMSELVES IN FRONT OF A BUS OR SOMETHING. EVEN THEY DIDN'T WANT TO BE AROUND HIM. NOBODY DOES.
ISN'T THAT RIGHT, "PETEY"?
SHUT UP, FLASH.
WHAT DID YOU SAY??
UNH!
HEY!
LEAVE HIM ALONE!
YOU! YOU'RE THOMPSON, RIGHT? EUGENE?
YOUR PARENTS WILL BE HEARING FROM ME WHEN I GET HOME!
HE STARTED IT!
YOU ALL RIGHT, PETEY?

WHY DID YOU DO THAT, UNCLE BEN?!

WHAT?

THEY USUALLY GET BORED AND *LEAVE ME ALONE*.

NOW-- YOU--

PETER--

I'LL *NEVER* BE ABLE TO LIVE THIS DOWN! THEY'LL *NEVER* LEAVE ME ALONE NOW!

*JUST GO AWAY!!*

PETER!

"AND NOW A BRIEF DEMONSTRATION OF HOW WE EXPERIMENT WITH RADIATION HERE IN THE LAB."

IONIZATION CAN CAUSE CANCER IN LIVING CELLS--

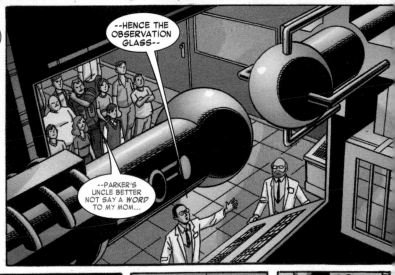

--HENCE THE OBSERVATION GLASS--

--PARKER'S UNCLE BETTER NOT SAY A *WORD* TO MY MOM...

IF I GET GROUNDED, THAT GEEK'S GONNA PAY FOR THE REST OF THE YEAR--

--BUT IT'S ALSO BEEN KNOWN TO CAUSE SOME... *ANOMALIES.*

WE EXPERIMENT WITH BACTERIA, FUNGI, INSECTS, *ARACHNIDS--*

--TRYING TO *CREATE* THESE ANOMALIES ON A SMALL SCALE, TO FIND OUT *WHY* THEY OCCUR.

--I SAY WE GIVE HIM A LITTLE *WARNING NOW,* IF YOU KNOW WHAT I MEAN-

VZZT.

VZZT!

ANYONE HERE EVER HEAR OF THE HULK--

WAIT! SOMETHING SEEMS TO BE--

GET BACK!

VZZT!

SKRASSSHHHH

AHH!

OWW!

ARE YOU OKAY, SON? COME ON.

STAY CLOSE, EVERYONE. WE'RE CALLING THE PARAMEDICS TO--

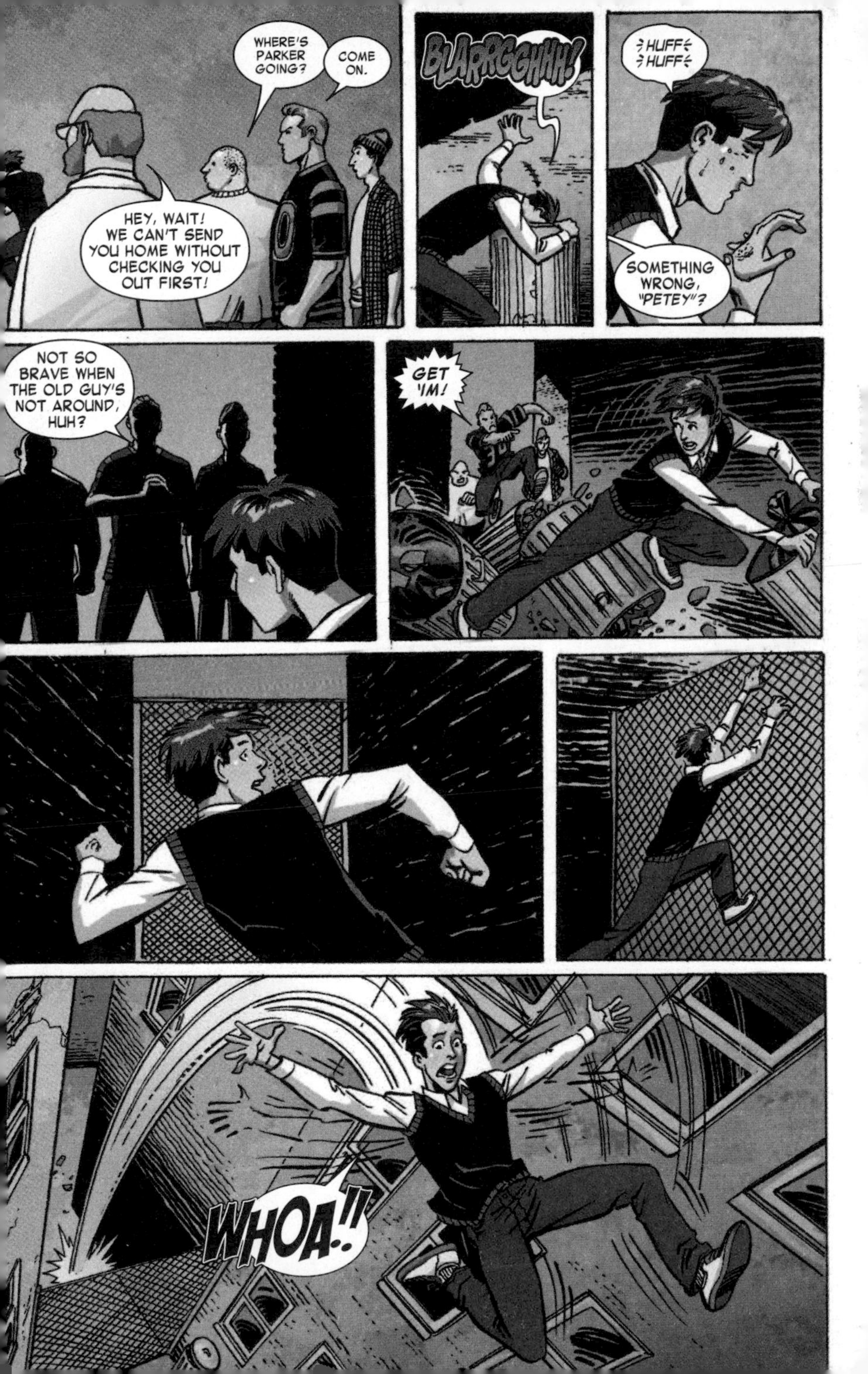
WHERE'S PARKER GOING?
COME ON.
HEY, WAIT! WE CAN'T SEND YOU HOME WITHOUT CHECKING YOU OUT FIRST!
BLARRGGHHH!
HUFF HUFF
SOMETHING WRONG, "PETEY"?
NOT SO BRAVE WHEN THE OLD GUY'S NOT AROUND, HUH?
GET 'IM!
WHOA..!!

WH-WHERE'D HE GO?

HE COULDN'T HAVE GOTTEN TOO FAR. C'MON, FLASH!

FLASH! COME ON!

WHAT JUST HAPPENED?!

PETEY?!

THANK GOODNESS! MR. DITKO CALLED HOURS AGO--

--NO ONE WAS SERIOUSLY INJURED IN THE EXPLOSION, BUT--

I'M FINE I'M GOING T'BED. 'NIGHT!

WAS IT THE SPIDER?

THE RADIATION?

BOTH?

MAYBE I'M ONE OF THOSE ANOMALIES OR--

OHMYGOD, AM I DYING?!

PETEY, CAN YOU OPEN THE DOOR, SON?

NO, CAN'T BE DYING. I FEEL... GREAT!

I FEEL LIKE I CAN LIFT A MOUNTAIN!

AND THOSE OTHER THINGS I CAN DO--

IS IT JUST TEMPORARY?

WHATEVER! JUST WAIT 'TIL FLASH THOMPSON--

ARE YOU ALL RIGHT? DO YOU WANT TO TALK?

NO! GOTTA BE SMART. CAN'T TELL ANYONE.

THEY'LL PUT ME IN A LAB. STUDY ME LIKE A FREAK.

BUT STILL, THERE'S GOTTA BE A WAY--

I DON'T HAVE TO BE A NOBODY ANYMORE!

"AND THE CHALLENGER..."

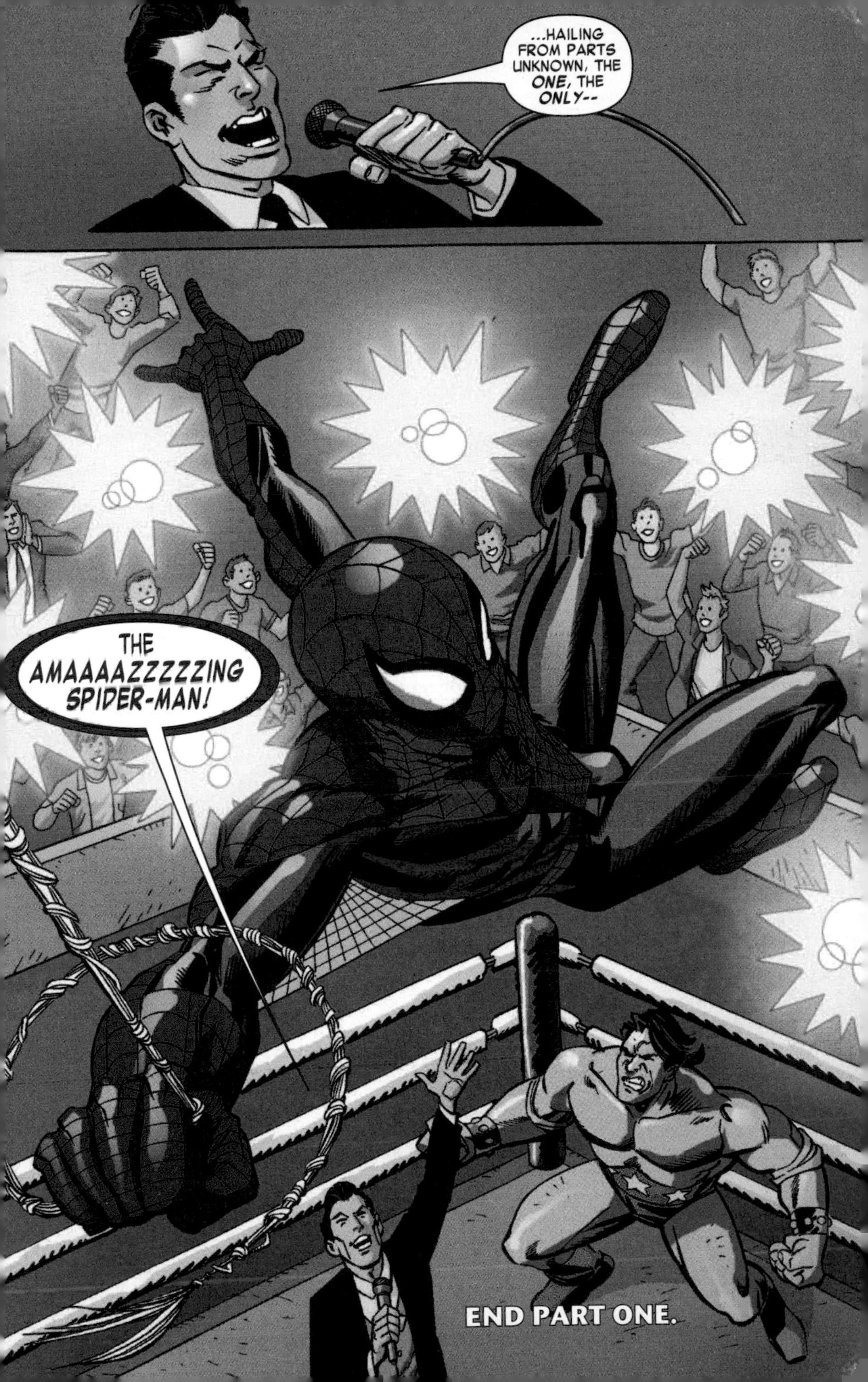
...HAILING FROM PARTS UNKNOWN, THE ONE, THE ONLY--
THE AMAAAAZZZZZZING SPIDER-MAN!
END PART ONE.

# PART TWO.

LOOK AT TROY, HE CAN'T EVEN *TOUCH* SPIDER-MAN!

LUCKY FOR HIM, 'CAUSE TROY'D MAKE HIM CHOKE ON THOSE WEBS!

PETER? YOUR AUNT MAY AND I ARE WATCHING THAT NEW WRESTLER GUY ON TV. WHY DON'T YOU COME DOWN?

PETER?

AND *"PRETTY BOY"* TROY IS DOWN!

OUCH! THAT'S *GOTTA* HURT!

PETER, I'VE SAID, *"I'M SORRY"* ABOUT A HUNDRED TIMES. IT'S BEEN WEEKS.

SOME DAY WHEN YOU HAVE YOUR OWN KIDS...

PETER PARKER, OPEN THIS DOOR RIGHT NOW!

TAKE IT EASY, KID!

BUT LOOK AT THEM! THEY'RE *EATING* IT UP!

I GUESS YOU NEED A LITTLE MORE TIME.

YOU MEAN EVERYTHING TO ME, PETER. I NEED YOU TO KNOW THAT.

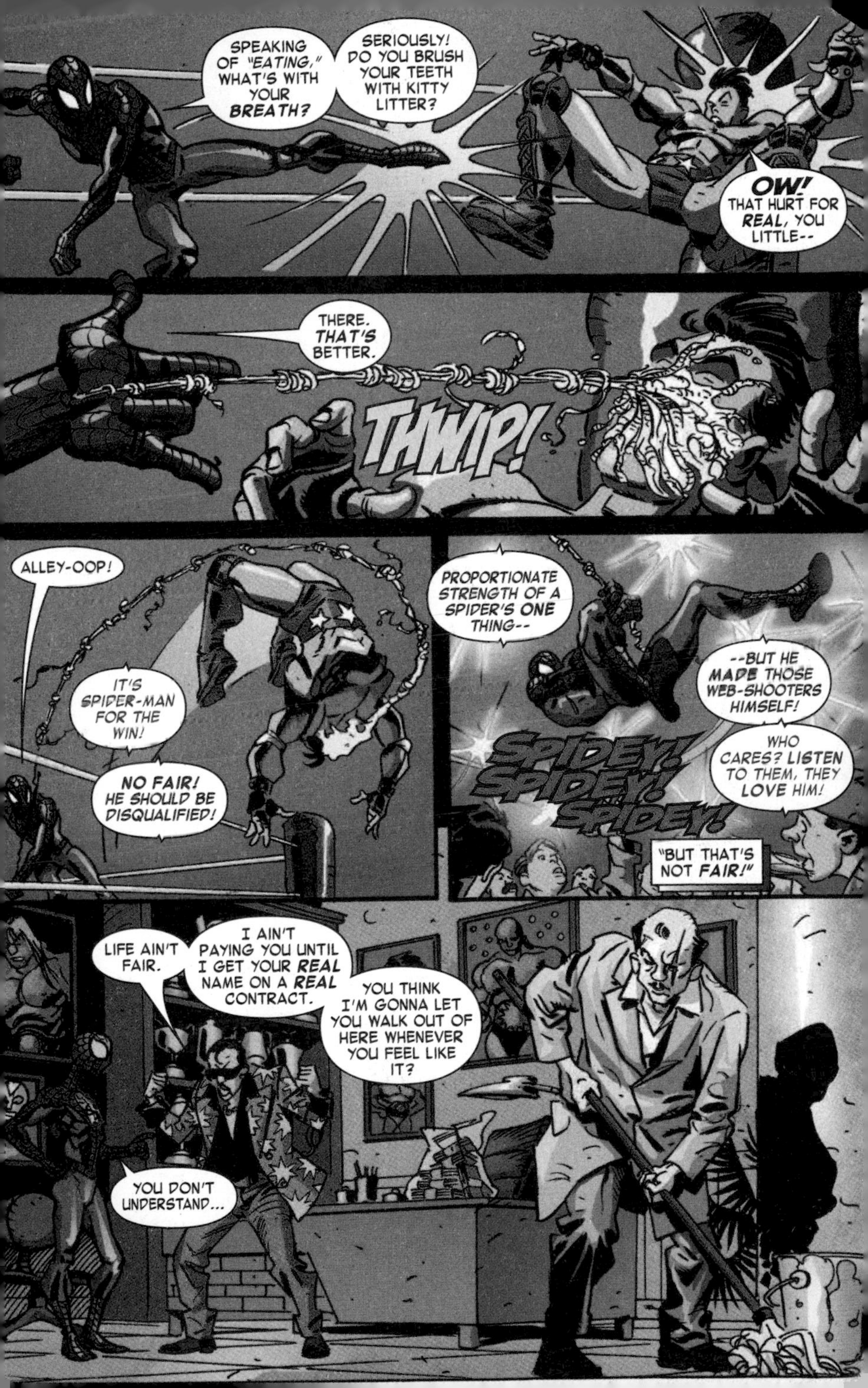
SPEAKING OF "EATING," WHAT'S WITH YOUR BREATH?
SERIOUSLY! DO YOU BRUSH YOUR TEETH WITH KITTY LITTER?
OW! THAT HURT FOR REAL, YOU LITTLE--
THERE. THAT'S BETTER.
THWIP!
ALLEY-OOP!
IT'S SPIDER-MAN FOR THE WIN!
NO FAIR! HE SHOULD BE DISQUALIFIED!
PROPORTIONATE STRENGTH OF A SPIDER'S ONE THING--
--BUT HE MADE THOSE WEB-SHOOTERS HIMSELF!
WHO CARES? LISTEN TO THEM, THEY LOVE HIM!
SPIDEY! SPIDEY! SPIDEY!
"BUT THAT'S NOT FAIR!"
LIFE AIN'T FAIR.
I AIN'T PAYING YOU UNTIL I GET YOUR REAL NAME ON A REAL CONTRACT.
YOU THINK I'M GONNA LET YOU WALK OUT OF HERE WHENEVER YOU FEEL LIKE IT?
YOU DON'T UNDERSTAND...

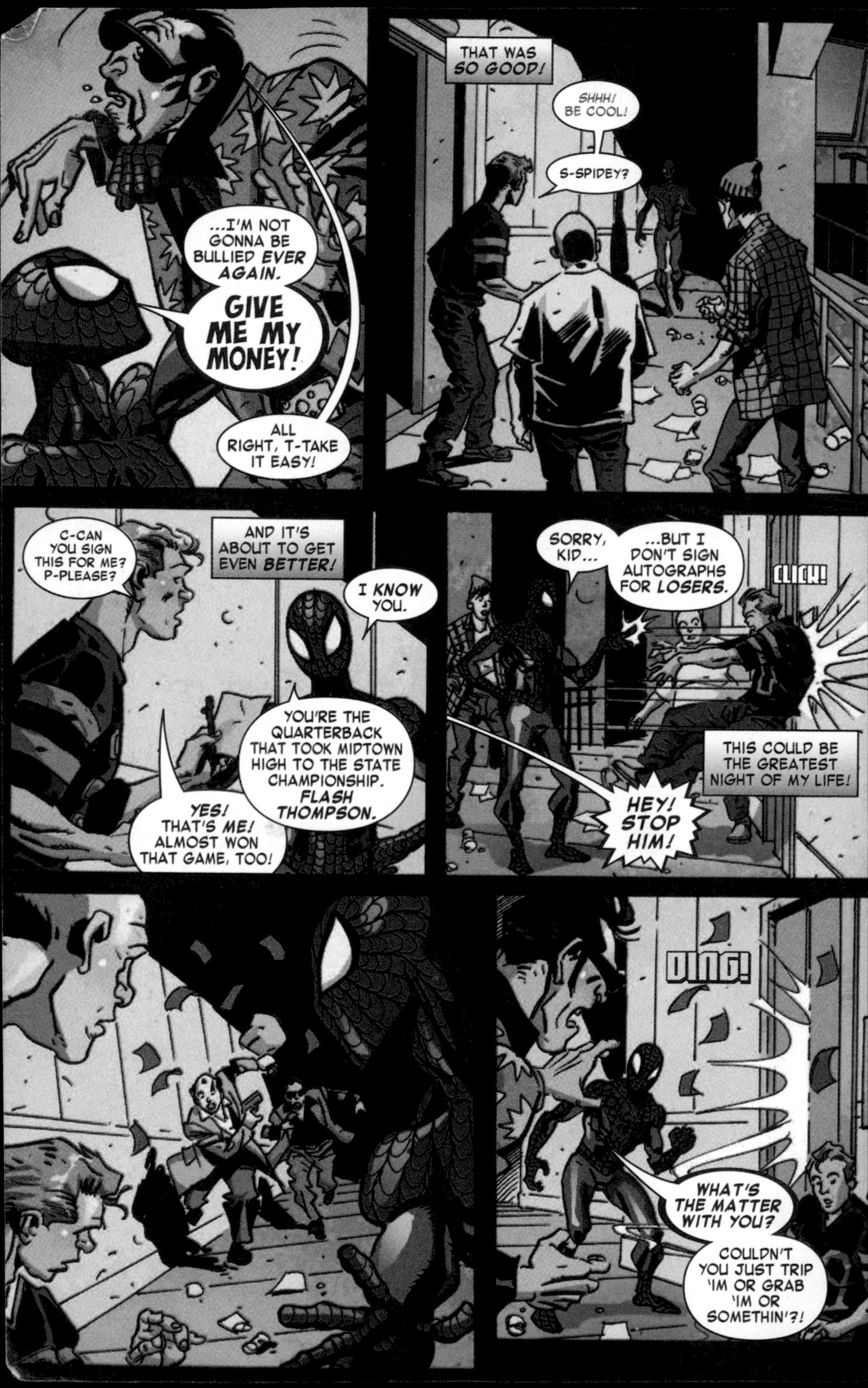

...I'M NOT GONNA BE BULLIED EVER AGAIN.
GIVE ME MY MONEY!
ALL RIGHT, T-TAKE IT EASY!
THAT WAS SO GOOD!
SHHH! BE COOL!
S-SPIDEY?
C-CAN YOU SIGN THIS FOR ME? P-PLEASE?
AND IT'S ABOUT TO GET EVEN BETTER!
I KNOW YOU.
YOU'RE THE QUARTERBACK THAT TOOK MIDTOWN HIGH TO THE STATE CHAMPIONSHIP. FLASH THOMPSON.
YES! THAT'S ME! ALMOST WON THAT GAME, TOO!
SORRY, KID...
...BUT I DON'T SIGN AUTOGRAPHS FOR LOSERS.
CLICK!
THIS COULD BE THE GREATEST NIGHT OF MY LIFE!
HEY! STOP HIM!
DING!
WHAT'S THE MATTER WITH YOU?
COULDN'T YOU JUST TRIP 'IM OR GRAB 'IM OR SOMETHIN'?!

WHAT'S THAT YOU SAID A MINUTE AGO?

OH YEAH, "LIFE AIN'T FAIR."

AND I'M NOT A COP.

YES, THIS IS *MOST DEFINITELY* THE GREATEST NIGHT OF MY LIFE.

UNCLE BEN WOULD BE SO PROUD!

I HAVEN'T BEEN ABLE TO LOOK HIM IN THE EYE SINCE--

--AND THE WAY I YELLED AT HIM...

I SHOULD DO SOMETHING NICE FOR HIM. BUY HIM A CAR OR SOMETHING.

HMM. HE'D WONDER WHERE I GOT THE MONEY.

SO WHAT? MAYBE I'LL JUST TELL HIM. SHARE MY SECRET.

HE'D PROBABLY GET A REAL KICK OUT OF IT--

HUH?

NO.

UNCLE BEN! AUNT MAY!

WHOA, YOU CAN'T GO IN THERE.

WHERE'S MY UNCLE?!

OH-- YOU'RE PETER!

WE'VE BEEN CALLING *ALL OVER* FOR YOU.

YOUR AUNT MAY IS *FINE*, SHE'S OVER AT THE WATSONS--

WHERE'S MY UNCLE?!

I'M SORRY, KID...

...YOUR UNCLE BEN'S *DEAD*.

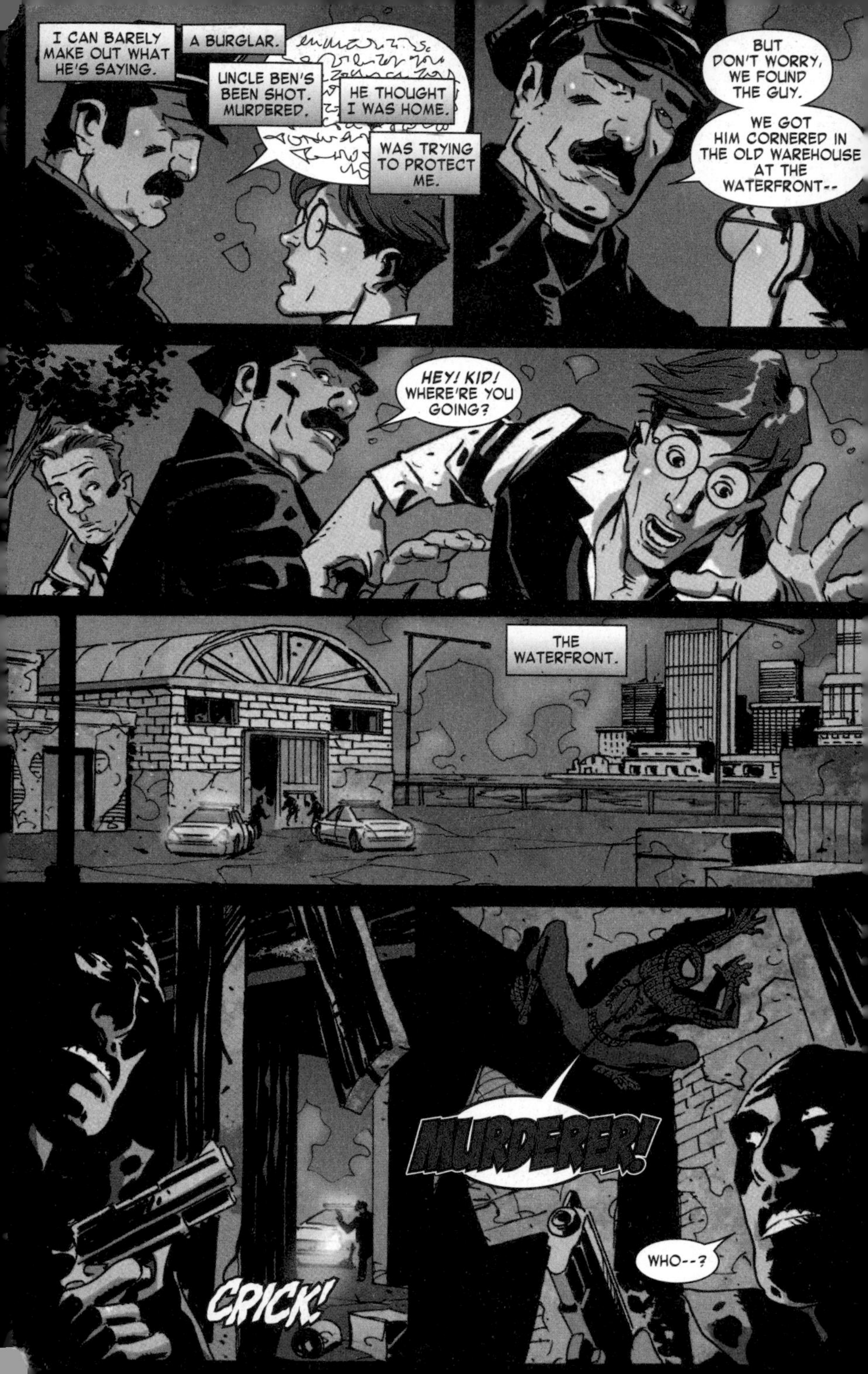
I CAN BARELY MAKE OUT WHAT HE'S SAYING.
A BURGLAR.
UNCLE BEN'S BEEN SHOT. MURDERED.
HE THOUGHT I WAS HOME.
WAS TRYING TO PROTECT ME.
BUT DON'T WORRY, WE FOUND THE GUY.
WE GOT HIM CORNERED IN THE OLD WAREHOUSE AT THE WATERFRONT--
HEY! KID! WHERE'RE YOU GOING?
THE WATERFRONT.
MURDERER!
WHO--?
CRICK!

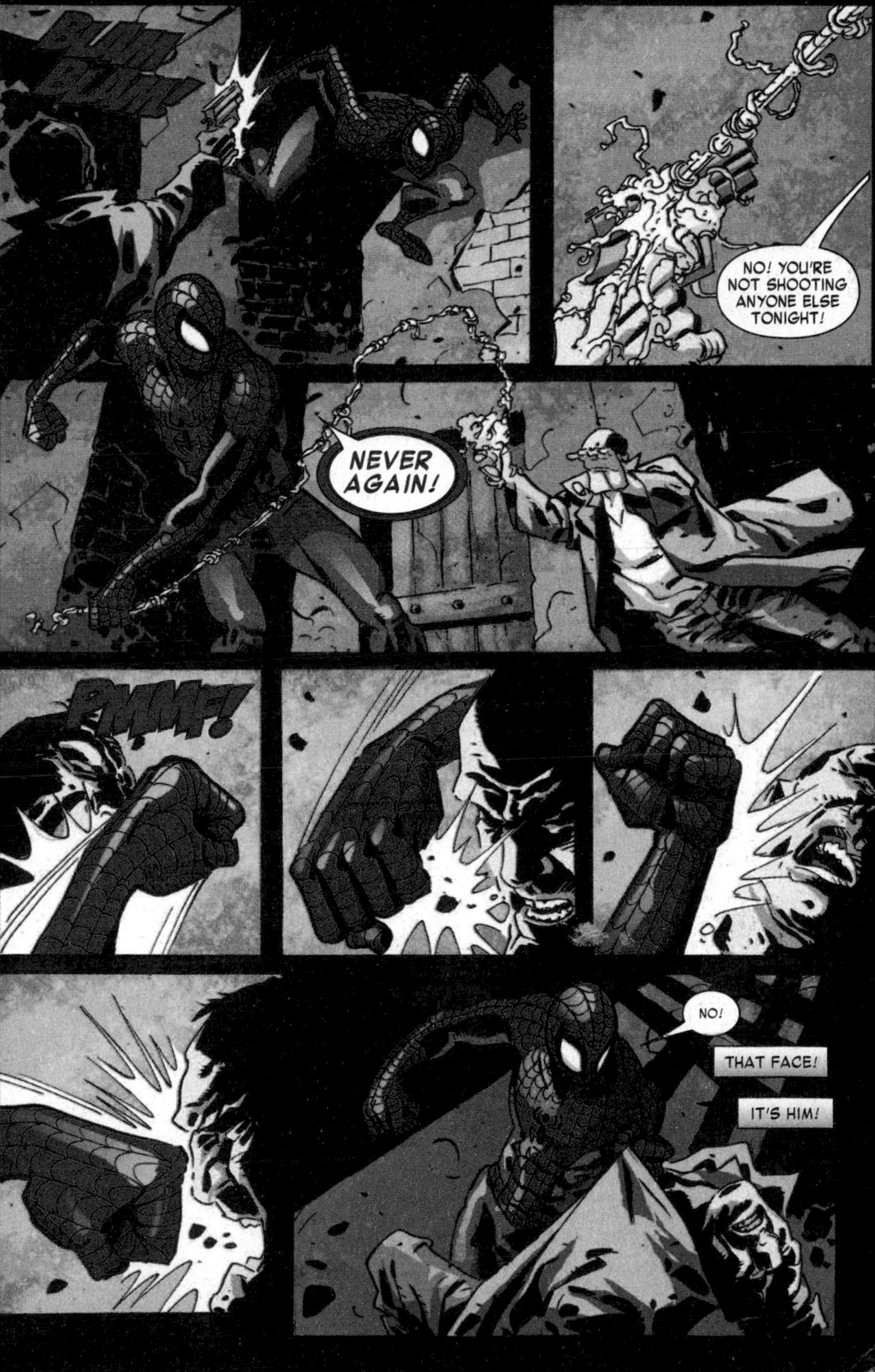
NO! YOU'RE NOT SHOOTING ANYONE ELSE TONIGHT!
NEVER AGAIN!
PMMF!
NO!
THAT FACE!
IT'S HIM!

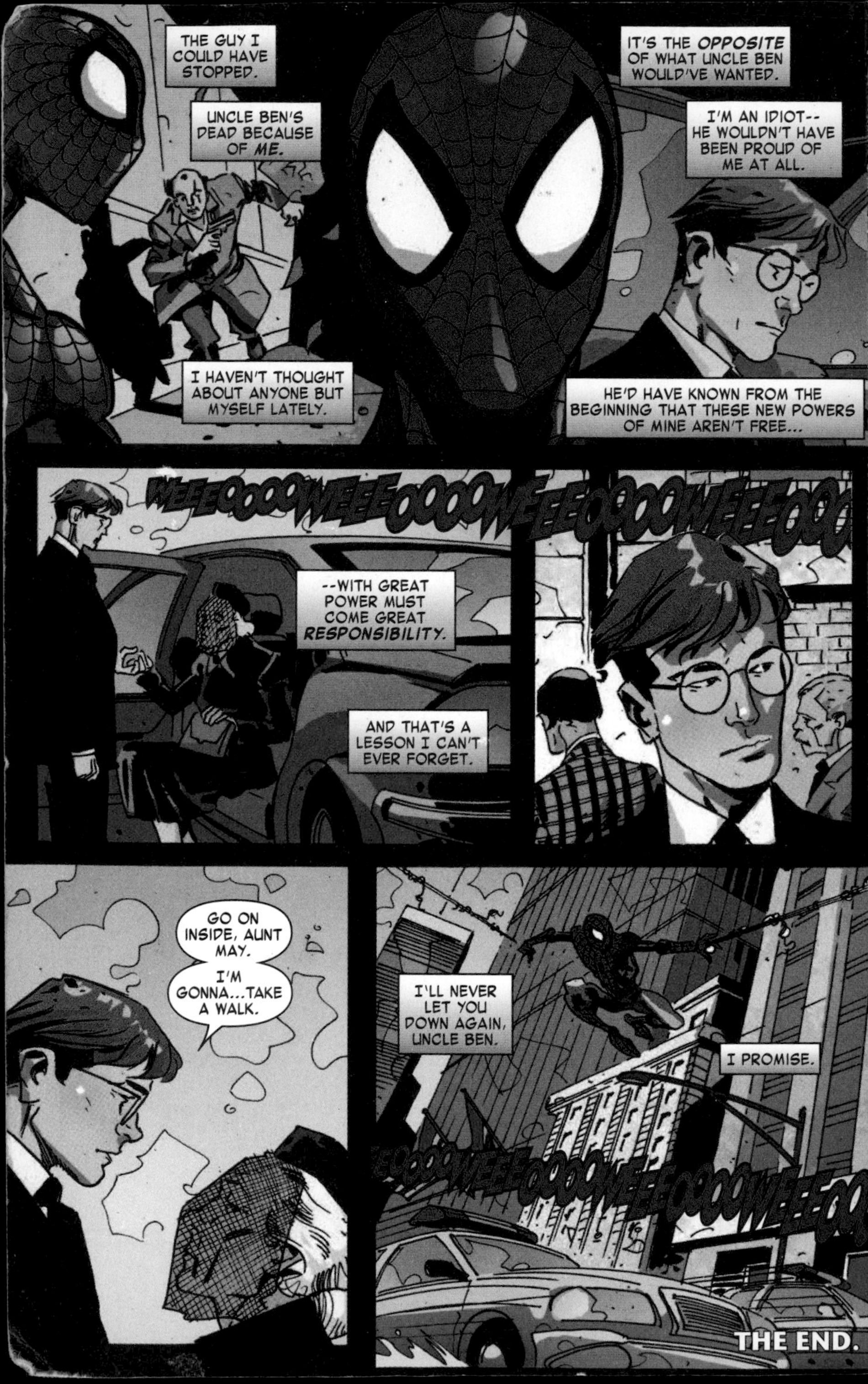
THE GUY I COULD HAVE STOPPED.
UNCLE BEN'S DEAD BECAUSE OF *ME.*
I HAVEN'T THOUGHT ABOUT ANYONE BUT MYSELF LATELY.
IT'S THE *OPPOSITE* OF WHAT UNCLE BEN WOULD'VE WANTED.
I'M AN IDIOT-- HE WOULDN'T HAVE BEEN PROUD OF ME AT ALL.
HE'D HAVE KNOWN FROM THE BEGINNING THAT THESE NEW POWERS OF MINE AREN'T FREE...
WEEEOOOOWEEEOOOOWEEEOOOOWEEEOOO
--WITH GREAT POWER MUST COME GREAT *RESPONSIBILITY.*
AND THAT'S A LESSON I CAN'T EVER FORGET.
GO ON INSIDE, AUNT MAY.
I'M GONNA...TAKE A WALK.
I'LL NEVER LET YOU DOWN AGAIN, UNCLE BEN.
I PROMISE.
EOOOOWEEEOOOOWEEEOOOOWEEEOO
THE END.